Feb 2020

Major League SOCCER

LA Galaxy

Tammy Gagne

Mitchell Lane
PUBLISHERS

2001 SW 31st Avenue
Hallandale, FL 33009

www.mitchelllane.com

Printing   1   2   3   4   5   6   7   8

Designer: Ed Morgan
Editor: Sharon F. Doorasamy

Library of Congress Cataloging-in-Publication Data

Names: Gagne, Tammy, author.
Title: LA Galaxy / by Tammy Gagne.Other titles: Los Angeles Galaxy
Description: Hallandale, FL : Mitchell Lane Publishers, 2019. | Series: Major League Soccer |
   Includes bibliographical references and index.
Identifiers: LCCN 2018003127| ISBN 9781680202601 (library bound) | ISBN 9781680202618 (ebook)
Subjects: LCSH: Los Angeles Galaxy (Soccer team)—History—Juvenile literature.
Classification: LCC GV943.6.L68 G36 2018 | DDC 796.334/640979494—dc23
LC record available at https://lccn.loc.gov/2018003127

Contents

Words in **bold** throughout
can be found in the Glossary.

The World's Most Popular Sport

The Los Angeles Galaxy and the New England Revolution had both made it all the way to the battle for the top soccer title in the United States—the Major League Soccer (MLS) Cup. The score was tied 1 to 1 when the game went into overtime. Gyasi Zardes had scored the Galaxy's first point in the 52nd minute, matched by New England's Chris Tierney in the 79th. LA forward Robbie Keane hadn't done much in the game yet, but that was about to change in a big way. His first and only goal of the game brought the silver trophy home for his team for the fifth time.

With more than 3.5 billion fans, soccer is the most popular sport in the world. Americans have been slow to embrace this athletic pastime, which began in England in 1883. By the early 1900s, soccer had become popular in Asia, Australia, and South America. Beginning in 1930, people around the globe celebrated when their country's team won the World Cup. Still, people in the United States seemed uninterested—until a Brazilian player called Pelé came to New York in 1975. His amazing skills introduced many US fans to the sport. Still, it would be more than 20 years before the United States would start its own national soccer league.

Pelé (*center*) in a game against S.L. Benfica in New York, August 1966

Chapter One

Major League Soccer

In 1996, after several years of planning, a national soccer league became a reality in the United States. MLS began with just 10 teams, but it grew quickly thanks to enthusiastic support from fans. Today the league includes 22 teams—19 in the United States and 3 in Canada. MLS divides its teams into two divisions, Eastern and Western. Teams in each division play one another during the regular season, which runs from March to October. During this time each team plays a total of 34 games, 17 at home and 17 away.

The top 12 teams—6 from each division—move on to the playoff season, which consists of 17 additional games. At the end of this process, the top team from each division moves on to play the other in the annual MLS Cup game. The winner of that game receives the MLS Cup title and trophy.

It Takes Many Nations

MLS is the most diverse professional sports league in North America. Although more than half the players came from the United States and Canada, the remaining team members, which amounted to 42.8 percent in 2015, came from a wide variety of nations around the world. That year, the 551 MLS players came from 58 different countries.

The most common foreign nations of origin for MLS players at this time were Argentina and the United Kingdom. Half of the MLS teams began the 2017 season with at least one Argentine player on their **rosters**, or lists of team members. In addition to their high numbers on the field, Argentine players also have the second-highest goal total in the league.

Foreign players come to the United States for many reasons, including money and the cultural experience. For players coming from poorer parts of the world, a regular paycheck is enough of a draw. But the high playing standard also tops the list for many players coming to the United States from other nations.

At his first Galaxy press conference, British player Steven Gerrard shared, "The MLS has grown and improved over the years, and the teams have also got stronger and better. I have been very impressed with the standard of training so far and I am certainly looking forward to playing against the other teams."

Fun Facts

1 Robbie Keane's game-changing shot earned him the title of Most Valuable Player in the 2014 MLS Cup game.

2 The winning team must give this original MLS Cup trophy back to the MLS headquarters during the off-season. They receive a **duplicate** trophy in return.

The Birth of the Galaxy

North America's excitement for the game of soccer skyrocketed during the mid-1990s. The United States hosted the World Cup for the first time in 1994. The monthlong event took place in nine US cities between June and July of that year. After record interest in the sport, the United States was in the process of establishing a professional soccer league for men. The Los Angeles Galaxy was one of the original teams in this league known as Major League Soccer. Founded in 1994, the Galaxy hoped to play its first season in the spring of 1995. It took a bit longer than planned to get the operation off the ground, however.

The LA Galaxy played their first game on April 13, 1996, at the Rose Bowl in Pasadena, California. They won the match against the MetroStars, 2–1. This team from New York and New Jersey would eventually change its name to the Red Bulls. Founding Galaxy players Cobi Jones and Arash Noamoaz scored the two goals on this historic day. The Rose Bowl would be the site of many more Galaxy victories that initial season. This stadium just outside Los Angeles remained the team's home turf until 2003.

The team's colors and logo would also change over time. The first Galaxy uniform was

Arash Noamouz (*right*) of the LA Galaxy and New York/New Jersey MetroStars player Mickey Kydes fight for the ball during a game in 1996.

black and teal with red and gold accents. The original team logo was made up of a gold swirl and teal letters with black and white outlines. The designs of both the uniform and the logo changed dramatically in 2007 when the team colors transformed into white, navy blue, and gold. The logo's swirl design was replaced with a blue shield bordered in gold. For the 2017 season, Galaxy players wore solid navy with white and gold lettering for away games and white with navy and gold diagonal stripes when playing at home.

The Home Field

The Galaxy's current home is the StubHub Center on the campus of California State University, in Dominguez Hills. Anschutz Entertainment Group (AEG), the company that also owns the LA Galaxy team, built this $150-million stadium which seats up to 27,000 soccer fans. It opened June 1, 2003 and hosted the MLS All-Star Game, the MLS Cup, and the FIFA Women's World Cup championship match during its first year. Today, in addition to the Galaxy games, the StubHub Center is the training site for the United States Soccer Federation Men's and Women's National Teams. It also serves as a **venue** for other sporting events and music concerts.

The LA Galaxy has a huge fan following, as evidenced by the team's attendance **statistics**. In 2012, the Galaxy's home games sold out six times. The average attendance fell from 23,136 in 2012 to 21,770 in 2013, but the drop was neither significant nor unexpected. Some fans worried that David Beckham's retirement that year would lower attendance much more than this small decrease. Although the numbers dropped to 21,258 in 2014, the 2015 season brought a new record high for average attendance—23,392. And attendance at the team's home games has kept rising since then. In 2016, the average attendance shot up to 25,147. Out of the 22 teams that are now part of MLS, the Galaxy came in fifth on the list for the highest attendance for this season.

Fans hold up signs for David Beckham as the Galaxy take on the Houston Dynamo in the MLS Cup in December 2012.

In 1996, the Galaxy became the first Western Conference champions in the brand-new Major Soccer League. Although the team was the favorite going into the MLS Cup that year, the Galaxy ended up losing to D.C. United. The team continued to dominate their regular seasons, making it all the way to the MLS Cup again in 2001, but they wouldn't take the big prize for the first time for another year.

Ricjie Williams of the D.C. United (*right*) moves the ball away from Cobi Jones of the Los Angeles Galaxy during the Major League Soccer MLS Championship game in October 1996.

Today the Galaxy hold the record for the most MLS wins in the history of the league, becoming the champions in 2002, 2005, 2011, 2012, and 2014. The only other team to come close to this record is D.C. United, with four wins under their belt. The Galaxy's most recent MLS Cup victory had the same score as the team's very first match so many years earlier, but this time the 2-to-1 win was over the New England Revolution.

Fun Facts

1 The team was named the Galaxy because Los Angeles is home to so many celebrities—or stars.

2 In 2014, AEG and the LA Galaxy founded a reserve team. Called the Galaxy II, they compete against other second-tier teams in MLS.

3 The team has a second uniform that they wear if the opposing team's uniform is too similar to the Galaxy's. Like their away uniform, this one is mostly blue.

Out of This World Action

In soccer, the athletes who play the offensive positions often get most of the glory. After all, it is these players who score the goals. Scoring is just one part of this complex sport, however.

As many coaches will tell you, a good offense begins with a strong defense.

One of the most vital defensive players on the field is the goalkeeper, or goalie. This person who stands in front of the net is the only player allowed to touch the ball with hands. Even with this privilege, stopping a ball that comes hurtling toward the net is often a challenging task. The players who can perform this task reliably are some of the truly most valuable in the game.

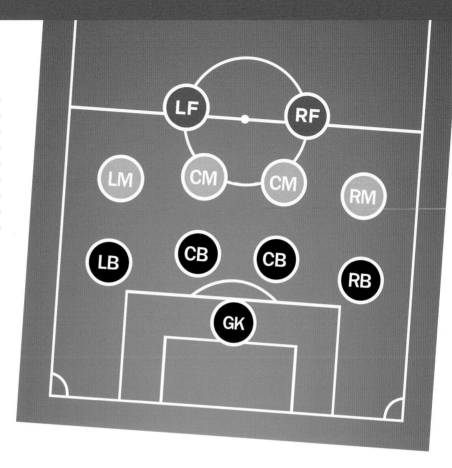

Goalkeeper(GK)
Right back defender (RB)
Left back defender (LB)
Center back defender (CB)
Left midfielder (LM)
Center midfielder (CM)
Right midfielder (RM)
Left forward (LF)
Right forward (RF)

Other defensive players include defensive midfielder, left back, right back, **stopper**, and **sweeper**. What these positions share is the duty to stop the opposing team's offense from getting the ball within range of the net. The stopper remains close to the net, trying to block an opponent from scoring. The sweeper also stays back, but his main job is to look for holes in his team's defense and move to cover them.

The offensive positions include the **striker**, forward, right midfielder, and left midfielder. The striker's main job is scoring goals. The forward helps the striker by passing the ball, but this position is also a common one for scoring. Both offensive midfielders also spend a fair amount of time passing. In the event of an opening, they may also make shots on the goal.

Cozmo, the mascot of the LA Galaxy, takes a selfie with fans prior to the Los Angeles Galaxy versus FC Barcelona game in July 2015.

Finally, every team needs a mascot, a character that embodies the spirit of the team and helps fans cheer for the players. The Galaxy's mascot is Cozmo. The team's official website claims that this alien fell to Earth in 2003 after he "made an emergency left turn to avoid a cow jumping over the moon" and began spiraling out of control. When he landed in Carson, California, Cozmo wanted to try out for the team, but because MLS players must be human, he was given the role of mascot instead. Many Galaxy fans see Cozmo as a lucky charm, since the team has won four of their five MLS Cup titles since his arrival.

The Galaxy's Biggest Rivalries

While every opponent may be called a rival, some teams are bigger competition than others. Some opponents also bring out the players' most competitive nature. One of the Galaxy's biggest rivalries is as old as MLS itself. The San Jose Earthquakes are a fellow California team, but this fact may only make the rivalry more intense. Each city, which is only 400 miles from the other, thinks its team is the best. Between 2001 and 2005, each team won the MLS Cup twice. When San Jose midfielder Landon Donovan moved to the Galaxy, this rivalry heated up even more. Many Earthquake fans saw him as a traitor while some Galaxy fans were slow to welcome the new player.

The Galaxy's rivalry with D.C. United also goes back to the beginning of the league. This is the team, after all, that took that first-ever MLS Cup away from the Galaxy. In 1999, the two teams faced each other once again at this event, and once again, D.C. walked away with the title. While this rivalry has softened as more teams have been added to the league, the fierce competition will never be forgotten. And as any LA player will point out, the Galaxy has the bragging rights of winning one more MLS title than D.C. United.

Today the Galaxy's biggest rival might just be the Seattle Sounders. This team from the state of Washington has its own in-state rivalry with the Portland Timbers. But its competitiveness with LA is also fairly strong. In one of the most exciting playoff games in the history of MLS, the Galaxy beat Seattle on their way to the 2014 MLS Cup. A goal by Juninho Pernambucano bounced off the goal post and into the net instead of out of it.

The Home Field Advantage

People have long believed that the team playing on their home field has an advantage of sorts. MLS statistics actually back up this belief. The league's teams have had a higher winning ratio at home than when playing on their opponents' fields. When the games are part of a playoff series, the advantage appears to be even greater. National data also supports the home-field theory.

Part of the reason may be that the home team has more support from fans. Having a crowd cheering instead of jeering inspires confidence. But a technical advantage may also figure into the equation. Although professional soccer fields are built to be as similar as possible, each one is certainly a bit different. Playing in a warmer or dryer climate is also a completely different experience. When players are used to one field or atmosphere, they will need time to get used to a new place. Since this adjustment can take time, those differences can decrease the visiting players' focus and ability.

The Journey to the Top

A Fox Sports article about the LA Galaxy from April of 2017 began, "The LA Galaxy have had a very un-Galaxy-like start to the 2017 season." While this opening line is far from a compliment, it shows the clear reputation that the team has made for itself over the years. People expect the Galaxy to win—and win often. The team's five MLS Cup titles are undeniably impressive. But it is how the Galaxy reached this incredible destination so many times that is most inspiring.

Some of the best teams are known for their talented offense. Others win numerous games because of their incredible defense. The Galaxy's powerhouse reputation comes from the fact that they excel at both. For 2017, Gyasi Zardes and Giovani dos Santos are among the team's most capable offensive players. And defenders Ashley Cole and Jelle Van Damme are on that ball when it slips past their offensive team members' feet. Historically, this important balance is what has taken the Galaxy to the top of the MLS ladder so many times.

Fun Facts

1 On July 4, 2016, Cozmo parachuted into the StubHub Center before the Galaxy's game against the Vancouver Whitecaps.

2 In 2005, the original San Jose Earthquakes moved to Texas to become the Houston Dynamos. San Jose returned with a new team roster in 2008.

The Stars of the Galaxy

Since the team's founding, the LA Galaxy have included some of the most gifted soccer players in the world. Some of these athletes have hung up their cleats and moved on to other pursuits while others are still in the game. Each one has made a mark on the team and on soccer itself.

Cobi Jones

A founding member of the team, Cobi Jones played for the LA Galaxy for 12 years. During this time he became one of their biggest assets. The team could depend on him for his excellent offense. He was also one of the Galaxy's most **versatile** players. He could play the forward position on both sides of the midfield. When he retired in 2007, he was the Galaxy's all-time leading scorer.

In an interview with *World Soccer Talk*, Jones shared which of his many victories means the most to him. "For me, it is the winning our first MLS Cup. We had been there 3 times before, and there was a lot of disappointment and pressure mounted to win it. It was an incredible moment for me—especially since I was captain."

David Beckham

Many people would argue that David Beckham is the best-known LA Galaxy player of all time. He is also often credited with growing American interest in the game of soccer. Beckham began playing full time for Manchester United in his native United Kingdom when he was just 20 years old. The gifted midfielder joined the La Galaxy in 2007. His five-year deal for $250 million made headlines everywhere. Beckham helped bring home two MLS Cups for the Los Angeles team before retiring in 2012. Although his days of playing professional ball are behind him, he remains one of the biggest names in the sport.

David Beckham on the field in 2010

Chapter Four

In 2016, Beckham told *GQ* magazine that he misses soccer every day. He confided, "If I was still living in L.A., I'd probably really seriously think about coming back for a year . . . I always think that I can step back on the field and play. Even now, at 40 years old, I still look at the national team and think, *I could do that!* . . . Even at 50, 60 years old, I'll be looking at the national team and thinking, *I can still do it!* . . . My friends are always honest with me: When I say I have an itch to come back and play again, they say, 'Just scratch it and shut up!'"

Giovani dos Santos

The LA Galaxy signed Giovani dos Santos in 2015. A strong midfielder and forward known for speed, he was already well known in his native Mexico by this time. Dos Santos first played for the Mexican national team when he was just 18 years old. By the time he was 25, he had played in the FIFA World Cup twice—in 2010 and 2014. In his first season with the Galaxy, he scored 14 goals and 12 **assists** in the regular season. He racked up another goal and assist during the playoffs.

When Fox Sports asked dos Santos about his biggest challenge, he quickly responded that it was staying in the elite. "[E]very day I focus, to work hard, to take care of myself, to take care of my body. You know, soccer is a short—how do you say . . . career! It's a short career, so I always try to focus, and I want to be in the elite for a long time . . . I see myself in the Galaxy. I want to stay for a long time."

Giovani dos Santos in May 2017

Fun Facts

1 After his retirement as a player, Cobi Jones went on to work as an assistant coach for the LA Galaxy until 2011.

2 David Beckham is best known for his ability to "bend" his kicks around opposing players. This difficult move inspired the phrase "Bend it like Beckham."

3 During his first season with the Galaxy, Giovani dos Santos was selected to play in the 2016 All-Star Game.

All about Communication

CHAPTER FIVE

The game of soccer is played in numerous countries throughout the world. Many of the best players hail from foreign nations. To field the best possible teams, MLS teams invite many players from these countries to join their rosters in the United States. In March of 2018, the Galaxy signed United Manchester's Zlatan Ibrahimovic. The Swedish footballer is one of the most famous players in the world and one of the greatest showmen the sport has ever seen.

In 2015, nearly half of all MLS players came from other nations. Among the most common countries of origin were Argentina, England, Brazil, Colombia, and France. Together players from just these five nations speak four different languages—Spanish, English, Portuguese, and French. How do players who do not speak the same language communicate with one another, their coaches, and their American teammates?

Many players insist that the spoken language barrier causes no issues on the field. Many parts of soccer rely on communication of a different kind entirely. Players watch each other's body language for hints about what they will do next. Learning to anticipate these moves is part of what makes the best soccer teams successful. A forward pushing the ball toward the opponent's net can certainly yell to the striker, "In ten seconds I'm going to use my left foot to kick the ball to your right side!" But sharing this information would obviously alert the other team's defense of the upcoming move.

Foreign players begin learning the English language immediately through a process called **immersion**. They are basically immersed into this new country with the majority of the people speaking English. They hear it all the time and learn the meaning of many words as they are repeated in the proper context. Many experts think that this method of learning a new language produces results as good as, if not better than, traditional foreign language study.

It is also important to note that US-born players are likely to pick up words in the foreign players' languages as well. Before a player from Argentina learns the English word goalie, he may call this teammate the *portero*. Likewise, a Brazilian player may refer to the soccer ball as the *bola de futebol*. If a player deserves a red card, a French player may yell, *carton rouge*. Just through everyday practice and play, the teammates from different countries may learn to use more than one spoken language on the field.

Adjusting to Playing in a New Country

Although many foreign players adjust quickly to playing the game with people who don't speak their native language, some find playing on an MLS team a big change in other ways. One of the hardest parts of playing in the United States can be the high amount of travel. Geographically, the United States is nine times larger than Colombia, for example. MLS players often spend more time traveling than they do on the training field.

Even the terrain and climate affect some players. After his 2015 season with the Galaxy, Steven Gerrard said how hard he found it to adjust to playing in the United States. The weather, the altitude, and even the playing surfaces were different than what he was used to back home in the United Kingdom.

MLS is also known to be incredibly demanding. Landon Donovan, who was born in California, noticed Gerrard's struggle. In 2015, Donovan told Goal.com, "As Gerrard said, it is difficult to adjust. I think David Beckham went through it too when he first came. For most people, the league is more difficult than they think. It's not necessarily better quality than where they come from but it is a very fast-paced, physical league. When you couple the traveling and the heat and different things, it makes it difficult."

Despite all its challenges, many foreign players are thriving playing soccer in the United States. Donovan pointed out that Galaxy forward Robbie Keane had an easy time adjusting after moving to Los Angeles from Ireland. "[H]e fit in straight away and didn't seem to miss a beat." Together with their US-born teammates, the players on the LA Galaxy and the 21 other MLS teams are inspiring young athletes all over the globe. And they are making the sport more popular than ever in North America.

Fun Facts

1 The 2017 LA Galaxy roster included players from Belgium, England, France, Germany, Ghana, Mexico, Portugal, and the United States.

2 About 3 million kids now play in US Youth Soccer leagues.

- The LA Galaxy team has been part of Major League Soccer since its creation.

- The Galaxy is part of the MLS's Western Division.

- The team plays at the StubHub Center on the campus of California State University, Dominguez Hills.

- The Galaxy have won the MLS Cup five times—in 2002, 2005, 2011, 2012, and 2014.

- The team's roster has included some of the biggest names in the sport. Cobi Jones, David Beckham, and Giovani dos Santos have all worn the Galaxy jersey.

- The Galaxy are known for both their offense and defense on the soccer field.

- The team's biggest rivals include the San Jose Earthquakes, D.C. United, and the Seattle Sounders.

- The Galaxy's official colors are white, navy blue, and gold.

- The team's mascot is an out-of-this-world character named Cozmo.

The Galaxy's Top Goals Scorers of the Regular 2016 Season

Giovani dos Santos: 14

Robbie Keane: 10

Gyasi Gardes: 6

Mike Magee: 6

1994
The LA Galaxy is founded.

1996
The team plays its first game against the MetroStars

2002
The Galaxy win their first MLS Cup title.

2003
The team moves from the Rose Bowl to its new home at the StubHub Center.

2005
The Galaxy become MLS Cup champions for the second time.

2007
David Beckham joins the LA Galaxy.

Cobi Jones retires from professional soccer, becomes an assistant coach for the Galaxy.

2011
The Galaxy win their third MLS Cup.

2012
The Galaxy become four-time MLS Cup champions.

David Beckham retires from professional soccer.

2014
The Galaxy set a record for the most MLS Cup wins after winning the title for the fifth time.

2015
The team signs Giovani dos Santos.
The Galaxy set a new record high for average attendance at their games–23,392.

Glossary

assist
A contribution by one player that results in another scoring a goal

duplicate
A copy of an original

immersion
The act of being placed in an environment to learn a language through constant exposure

roster
A list of team members

statistics
The collection and analysis of data

stopper
A defensive soccer player whose primary job is preventing the other team from scoring

striker
An offensive soccer player whose primary job is scoring goals

sweeper
A defensive soccer player whose primary job is preventing the other team from shooting on the goal

venue
The scene of an organized event such as a soccer game

versatile
Capable of performing a variety of tasks

Further Reading

Hoena, Blake. *Everything Soccer*. Washington, DC: National Geographic Children's Books, 2014.

Jokulsson, Illugi. *Stars of World Soccer*. New York: Abbeville Kids, 2015.

Osborne, Mary Pope. *Soccer*. New York: Random House, 2014.

On the Internet

LA Galaxy
https://www.lagalaxy.com/

LA Galaxy II
https://www.lagalaxy.com/2

Major League Soccer
https://www.mlssoccer.com/

Index

About the Author

Tammy Gagne is the author of numerous books for adults and children, including *Hope Solo* and *What It's Like to Be Pelé* for Mitchell Lane Publishers. She resides in northern New England with her husband and son. One of her favorite pastimes is visiting schools to speak to kids about the writing process.